THE OLD
FARMER'S ALMANAC

# Garden Journal

**NAME:**

---

**DATE:**

---

**LET MY WORDS, LIKE VEGETABLES,
BE TENDER AND SWEET,
FOR TOMORROW I MAY HAVE TO EAT THEM.**

–THOMAS ALOYSIUS "TAD" DORGAN, AMERICAN CARTOONIST (1877–1929)

WHERE A KITCHEN GARDEN GROWS, so grows food, health, joy, and knowledge. A vegetable plot is a slice of heaven on Earth, be it a pot of cucumbers on a doorstep, raised beds of onions and heirloom tomatoes, or row upon row of corn, beans, and squashes. As Alice B. Toklas wrote in her 1954 cookbook, "The first gatherings of the garden in May of salads, radishes, and herbs made me feel like a mother about her baby—how could anything so beautiful be mine. And this emotion of wonder filled me for each vegetable as it was gathered every year. There is nothing that is comparable to it, as satisfactory or as thrilling, as gathering the vegetables one has grown." Take a moment to reflect on the wonders and satisfactions of a garden, jot down ideas and observations, and make space to dream—of just-thawed dirt turning over at the request of your trowel, the sight of seedlings pushing up through the soil toward the Sun, a basketful of fresh, delicious, homegrown food. May each day spent in the garden be a gift to the mind, body, and soul, grounding us in cycles as old as the Earth and reminding us that we are naturally capable of new growth.

**OF ALL THE FLOWERS IN THE GARDEN, I LIKE THE CAULIFLOWER BEST.**

–DR. SAMUEL JOHNSON, ENGLISH WRITER (1709–84)

*Life begins the day you start a garden.*

–Chinese proverb

*This cabbage, these carrots, these potatoes,*
*these onions . . . will soon become me. Such a tasty fact!*

–Mike P. Garofalo, American poet (1943–2024)

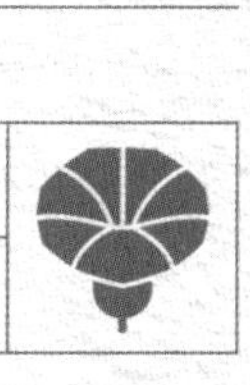

Use old salt and pepper shakers for sowing tiny seeds.
Mix with sand for better spreading.

WHEN FLOWERS BLOOM,
I HOPE YOU'LL NOT SNEEZE,
AND MAY YOU ALWAYS HAVE
SOMEONE TO SQUEEZE.

–IRISH BLESSING

*Every insect has a mortal enemy. Cultivate that enemy, and he will do your work for you.*

–Eleanor Perényi, American writer (1918–2009), in *Green Thoughts: A Writer in the Garden*

*As the garden grows, so does the gardener.*

–Unknown

*Gardening requires lots of water—*
*most of it in the form of perspiration.*
–Lou Erickson, American cartoonist (1913–90)

TO WELL-DRIED ROSE PETALS
AND SWEET BASIL, ADD DRIED MINT AND
POUNDED CLOVES. MIX WELL AND STUFF
A SMALL PILLOW WITH THE MIXTURE
TO INDUCE SLEEP AND FRAGRANT DREAMS.

–ELIZA SMITH, ENGLISH WRITER (DIED c. 1732)
IN *THE COMPLEAT HOUSEWIFE*

Pesto sauce will keep its bright color in pasta that is cooked with a few drops of lemon juice.

*When the root is deep, there is no reason to fear the wind.*

–African proverb

When planted next to tomatoes, basil is said to improve their flavor and vigor and to deter insects such as whiteflies.

**IF THERE WERE TO BE AN AWARD GIVEN FOR EXCELLENT DESIGN IN VEGETABLES, SURELY THE EGGPLANT WOULD BE DECLARED THE WINNER. ITS PERFECT OVOID SHAPE, ITS ROYAL-PURPLE SATIN SKIN, CROWNED WITH ITS VIBRANT GREEN CAP, ITS HEAVINESS IN THE HAND, ITS SENSUAL TOUCH, MAKES IT TRULY A VISUAL AND TACTILE DELIGHT.**

–SHERYL LONDON, AMERICAN WRITER,
IN *EGGPLANT AND SQUASH, A VERSATILE FEAST*

*If the Moon show a silver shield, be not afraid to reap your fields.*

–Weather lore

*About now, the potato bugs hold their annual convention . . . your cabbages, cauliflower, broccoli, tomatoes, eggplants, etc., will need watching, too.*

–*The Old Farmer's Almanac*, 1945

Start cooking root vegetables in cold water;
aboveground vegetables, in boiling water.

**HE LOVED TO SAUNTER THROUGH FIELDS OF WILD OATS AND CORNFLOWERS AND BUSIED HIMSELF WITH CLOUDS NEARLY AS MUCH AS WITH EVENTS.**

–VICTOR HUGO, FRENCH WRITER (1802–85), IN *LES MISÉRABLES*

For long-lasting blooms, pick flowers in the late afternoon when leaves and stems contain the most sugar.

*To forget how to dig the earth and to tend the soil is to forget ourselves.*

–Mahatma Gandhi, Indian spiritual leader (1869–1948)

*If you would enjoy the fruit, pluck not the flower.*

–English proverb

WE KNOW LITTLE ABOUT LOVE.
LOVE IS LIKE A PEAR.
A PEAR IS SWEET AND HAS A DISTINCT SHAPE.
TRY TO DEFINE THE SHAPE OF A PEAR.

–ANDRZEJ SAPKOWSKI, POLISH WRITER (B. 1948), IN *TIME OF CONTEMPT*

Plant fruit trees and bare-root plants as soon as the ground can be worked in the spring. This ensures they will have a long growing season to get established before winter arrives.

Pick pears while they are still green rather than waiting for them to ripen on the tree. Store the harvest in a cool (34° to 40°F) place for about a week. Then, bring fruit to room temperature for a few days before eating.

*A fruit is a vegetable with looks and money. Plus, if you let fruit rot, it turns into wine, something brussels sprouts never do.*

–P. J. O'Rourke, American writer (1947–2020)

**THE FRUIT IS NOT LONG OR ROUND, BUT ALTOGETHER BROADE, AND IN A MANNER FLAT LIKE ONTO A SHIELD OR BUCKLER; THICKER IN THE MIDDLE, THINNER IN THE COMPASSE, AND CURLED OR BUMPED IN CERTAIN PLACES ABOUT THE EDGES . . .**

–JOHN GERARD, ENGLISH HERBALIST (1545–1612), IN *THE HERBALL, OR, GENERALL HISTORIE OF PLANTES*

To slow decay, leave 1 to 2 inches of stem on pumpkins and winter squashes when harvesting them.

*A weed is a plant that has mastered every survival skill except for learning how to grow in rows.*

–Doug Larson, American writer (1926–2017)

When working in the garden, wrap a strip of flypaper around your hat and fasten it with a paper clip to catch swarming bugs.

**THAT WHICH ABOVE ALL YIELDS THE SWEETEST SMELL IN THE AIR IS THE VIOLET.**

–SIR FRANCIS BACON, ENGLISH STATESMAN (1561–1626)

*There was a time when a meticulously maintained lawn was a sign of affluence. If that were still the case, I would be considered impoverished. I love my lawn as it is: a colorful patchwork quilt of sunny yellow dandelions, white and purple violets, and fiery red hawkweed.*

–George Lohmiller, *The Old Farmer's Almanac*, 2012

*The Amen! of nature is always a flower.*

–Oliver Wendell Holmes, American writer and physician (1809–94), in "The Autocrat of the Breakfast-Table"

*We may pass violets looking for roses.*
*We may pass contentment looking for victory.*
–Bernard Williams, English writer (1929–2003)

**I PLANT ROSEMARY ALL OVER THE GARDEN, SO PLEASANT IS IT TO KNOW THAT AT EVERY FEW STEPS ONE MAY DRAW THE KINDLY BRANCHLETS THROUGH ONE'S HAND AND HAVE THE ENJOYMENT OF THEIR INCOMPARABLE INCENSE.**

–GERTRUDE JEKYLL, ENGLISH HORTICULTURALIST (1843–1932), IN *HOME AND GARDEN*

Rosemary plants will deter bean beetles
and carrot flies in the garden.

Burn a little sage or rosemary over coals to repel mosquitoes.

*Earth is here so kind, that just tickle her with a hoe and she laughs with a harvest.*

–Douglas Jerrold, English playwright (1803–57), in *A Land of Plenty*

**YOU NEED AN ENTIRE LIFE JUST TO KNOW ABOUT TOMATOES.**

–FERRAN ADRIA, SPANISH CHEF (B. 1962)

*The tomato hides its griefs. Internal damage is hard to spot.*

–Julia Child, American culinary expert (1912–2004)

*Gardening is cheaper than therapy—and you get tomatoes.*

–Unknown

*Of plants, tomatoes seemed the most human, eager and fragile and prone to rot.*

–John Updike, American writer (1932–2009), in *The Witches of Eastwick*

## HOW TO GARDEN IN HARMONY WITH OUR NEAREST CELESTIAL NEIGHBOR

Every 29.5 days or so, the Moon revolves around Earth. On each pass, depending on how much sun it reflects back to us, the Moon goes through phases, from new to full, then back to new. In its new phase, the Moon appears to go missing from the evening sky; when full, on clear nights, it is a bright disc illuminating the nighttime landscape.

During the new and full Moons, ocean tides are higher than at other times of the month. The gravity of the Moon's revolution impacts the movement of Earth's oceans—and everything else made of water, including humans, insects, plants, and soil. We are composed of about 60 percent water, and most species of plants are between 80 and 90 percent water, so it follows that as the Moon shifts ocean tides, living things respond to its influence, too.

A basic guideline for gardening by the Moon is to plant aboveground crops as the Moon is waxing (increasing from new to full) and plant belowground crops as the Moon is waning (decreasing from full to new).

### GET SOWING: NEW MOON TO FIRST QUARTER

- Sow plants that produce seeds outside the fruit, such as arugula, basil, broccoli, cabbage, grains, lettuce, radicchio, spinach, and most herbs.
- Prune for growth.
- Turn the soil for aeration when there is less moisture in it, making it easier to move.
- Harvest plants that produce leafy, fruity parts above ground during the Moon's waxing phase.

### GET GROWING: FIRST QUARTER TO FULL MOON

- Sow plants that produce their seeds inside the fruit, such as beans, melons, peas, peppers, squashes, and tomatoes.
- Graft trees close to the full Moon.

### GET ROOTED: FULL MOON TO LAST QUARTER

- Plant root crops the week following a full Moon.
- Transplant to establish roots.
- Prune to retain shape (versus encourage growth).
- Harvest belowground plants such as carrots and potatoes.

### GET GROUNDED: LAST QUARTER TO NEW MOON

- Pull weeds.
- Harvest, then dry, can, ferment, and pickle.
- Prune or mow for decreased growth.
- Take stock, review notes, refine ideas.

# COMPANION PLANTS

Companion planting is matchmaking in the garden. It's the traditional practice of growing certain plants together to increase their vitality, flavor, and ability to ward off pests.

While plants typically compete for available resources, we also know that many herbs, for instance, act as repellents, confusing insects with their strong odors that mask the scent of the host plants. Dill and basil protect tomatoes from hornworms, and sage reduces damage from cabbage worms. With just about any garden plant, marigolds repel beetles, nematodes, and even animal pests.

Some plant buddies act as traps, luring insects to themselves. Nasturtiums are so favored by aphids that the devastating insects flock to them. Carrots, dill, parsley, and parsnips attract ladybugs, praying mantises, and spiders that dine on insect pests.

Other companion plants are simply good neighbors. Lettuce, radishes, and other quick-growing crops sown between hills of melons or winter squashes will mature and be harvested long before these vines need more legroom. Leafy greens like spinach and Swiss chard grown in the shadow of corn or sunflowers appreciate the dappled shade provided, and because their roots occupy different levels in the soil, they do not compete for water and nutrients.

In contrast, plant foes can have detrimental effects. For example, although white garlic and onions repel a variety of pests and are companions to many plants, the growth of beans and peas is stunted in their presence. Potatoes and beans grow poorly in the company of sunflowers, and although cabbage and cauliflower are closely related, they don't like being planted near one another. It turns out companionship is just as important for gardens as it is for gardeners.

| CROP | FRIENDS | | | | FOES |
|---|---|---|---|---|---|
| **Beans** | Beets<br>Broccoli<br>Cabbage<br>Carrots | Cauliflower<br>Celery<br>Corn<br>Cucumbers | Eggplant<br>Peas<br>Potatoes<br>Radishes | Savory (S.)<br>Squashes<br>Strawberries<br>Tomatoes | Garlic<br>Onions<br>Peppers<br>Sunflowers |
| **Cabbage** | Beans<br>Celery<br>Cucumbers | Dill<br>Kale<br>Lettuce | Onions<br>Potatoes<br>Sage | Spinach<br>Thyme | Broccoli<br>Cauliflower<br>Strawberries<br>Tomatoes |
| **Carrots** | Beans<br>Lettuce<br>Onions | Parsley<br>Peas | Radishes<br>Rosemary | Sage<br>Tomatoes | Anise<br>Dill |
| **Corn** | Beans<br>Cucumbers | Lettuce<br>Melons | Peas<br>Potatoes | Squashes<br>Sunflowers | Tomatoes |
| **Cucumbers** | Beans<br>Cabbage | Cauliflower<br>Corn | Lettuce<br>Peas | Radishes<br>Sunflowers | Aromatic herbs<br>Melons<br>Potatoes |
| **Lettuce** | Asparagus<br>Beets<br>Brussels sprouts<br>Cabbage | Carrots<br>Corn<br>Cucumbers<br>Eggplant | Onions<br>Peas<br>Potatoes<br>Radishes | Spinach<br>Strawberries<br>Sunflowers<br>Tomatoes | Broccoli |
| **Onions** | Beets<br>Broccoli<br>Cabbage | Carrots<br>Lettuce | Peppers<br>Potatoes | Spinach<br>Tomatoes | Beans<br>Peas<br>Sage |
| **Peppers** | Basil<br>Coriander | Onions | Spinach | Tomatoes | Beans<br>Kohlrabi |
| **Radishes** | Basil<br>Beans | Carrots<br>Cucumbers | Lettuce<br>Peas | Spinach<br>Tomatoes | Hyssop<br>Kohlrabi |
| **Tomatoes** | Asparagus<br>Basil<br>Beans<br>Borage | Carrots<br>Celery<br>Dill<br>Lettuce | Melons<br>Onions<br>Parsley<br>Peppers | Radishes<br>Spinach<br>Thyme | Broccoli<br>Brussels sprouts<br>Cabbage<br>Cauliflower<br>Corn<br>Kale<br>Potatoes |

Harvesting at peak flavor is one of the joys of growing your own food. Harvest is derived from the Old English word *haerfest* (autumn), though it takes place during every season in North America. While there are rules of thumb, the correct timing and method for harvesting each crop differ slightly.

## HARVESTING BASICS

- Harvest in the early morning once the dew dries. This is when vegetables are at their juiciest and most flavorful. Produce will keep longer and not become limp from heat; this especially applies to leafy greens and herbs such as parsley and basil.
- Once a crop starts producing, check the garden daily. For instance, zucchini can quickly grow to 2 feet long, yet they are best at 6 to 8 inches.
- Bigger is not (usually) better. Big beans, beets, and okra pods will be tough and woody; too-big radishes turn into indigestible fiber.
- Be gentle. Pick with care. Stems and branches break easily, inviting disease. Use two hands to pick; hold the stem in one hand and pick with the other. If the crop is ripe but doesn't easily pull by hand (such as eggplant), use scissors, pruners, or a knife.
- Not all fruit and vegetables ripen the same way. Pears are picked when they are still hard. Cucumbers, squashes, and watermelons must be fully developed before being picked. Apples, peaches, and tomatoes can ripen on or off the vine.

Cut **ASPARAGUS** spears at the soil surface when they are firm, have closed tips, and are 6 to 8 inches long—before the base gets tough.

Harvest pole or snap **BEANS** by snipping or breaking the pod off from the stem above the cap. Pick every other day so they keep producing.

Harvest **PEPPERS** by cutting the stem; do not twist or break them off by hand. Sweet peppers can be eaten unripe (green) or ripe (orange, red, or yellow); they taste sweeter as they ripen. The more you pick, the more they produce.

Harvest **POTATOES** after the plants flower, 6 to 8 weeks after sowing. Once the foliage has died back, wait another couple of weeks for their skins to thicken. Dig 8 inches around plants to avoid damaging the potatoes.

Harvest **PUMPKINS** and **WINTER SQUASHES** on a dry day after the plants have died back; look for hard skins and full color. Cut the stem, leaving 2 inches to deter rotting. Cure in the sunshine (or a warm, dry room) for 10 days before storing in a cool, dry place.

For best flavor, leave **TOMATOES** on the vine as long as they remain firm. Look for fruit rich in color with smooth, glossy skin and a fragrant aroma. If frost is predicted, pick green tomatoes to ripen indoors.

THE MORNING GLORIES AND THE SUNFLOWERS
TURN NATURALLY TOWARD THE LIGHT,
BUT WE HAVE TO BE TAUGHT, IT SEEMS.

–FATHER RICHARD ROHR, AMERICAN WRITER (B. 1943)

To protect maturing sunflower seeds from hungry birds, cover the seed heads with cheesecloth.

Snapdragons bespeak presumption; sunflowers, haughtiness.

*A vegetable garden in the beginning looks so promising and then after all little by little it grows nothing but vegetables, nothing, nothing but vegetables.*

–Gertrude Stein, American writer (1874–1946), in *Wars I Have Seen*

**TO CREATE A GARDEN IS TO SEARCH FOR A BETTER WORLD. . . . WHETHER THE RESULT IS A HORTICULTURAL MASTERPIECE OR ONLY A MODEST VEGETABLE PATCH, IT IS BASED ON THE EXPECTATIONS OF A GLORIOUS FUTURE. THIS HOPE FOR THE FUTURE IS AT THE HEART OF ALL GARDENING.**

–MARINA SCHINZ, GERMAN PHOTOGRAPHER, IN *VISIONS OF PARADISE*

*A garden of spring and tender greens*
*and gold—the steady green of summer.*

–*The Old Farmer's Almanac*, 1958

Before the ground freezes, run a tiller through the vegetable garden to expose overwintering insects to freezing temperatures.

*Rain in spring is as precious as oil.*

–Chinese proverb

**GARDENS ARE THE RESULT OF A COLLABORATION BETWEEN ART AND NATURE.**

–PENELOPE HOBHOUSE, ENGLISH GARDEN WRITER AND DESIGNER (B. 1929)

Leave seed heads on asters, sunflowers, and cosmos for birds to eat over the winter.

*The philosopher who said that "work well done never needs doing over" never weeded a garden.*

–Ray D. Everson, American writer (c. 1884–1960)

*A gardener learns more in the mistakes than in the successes.*

–Barbara Dodge Borland, American writer (1903–91)

FROM ALL THESE TREES,
IN THE SALADS, THE SOUP, EVERYWHERE,
CHERRY BLOSSOMS FALL.

-MATSUO BASHO, JAPANESE POET (1644-94)

*Never make two bites at a cherry.*

–*The Old Farmer's Almanac*, 1793

Birch bark around your small peach and cherry trees will protect them from pests.

*A cherry year, a merry year.*

–English proverb

**FLAME-FLOWER, DAY-TORCH, MAUNA LOA,**
**I SAW A DARING BEE, TODAY, PAUSE, AND SOAR,**
**INTO YOUR FLAMING HEART.**

–ANNE SPENCER, AMERICAN POET (1882–1975),
IN "LINES TO A NASTURTIUM"

When pepper plants bloom, mix 1 tablespoon of Epsom salt in a gallon of water and then spray the solution on the plants. You will get larger plants and fruit.

Bury seaweed in garden soil: Root crops will love it.

*Plough deep and you will have plenty of corn.*

–Spanish proverb

A PICKLE IS A CUCUMBER WITH EXPERIENCE.

–IRENA CHALMERS, ENGLISH WRITER (1935–2020)

Rub a slice of cucumber on an ant bite.

Vertical vegetable gardening saves space and enables you to reach the harvest more easily. It also improves air circulation and prevents development of fungal diseases. Train climbing plants like cucumbers, pole beans, squashes, and tomatoes to grow up A-frames, arbors, cages, or trellises.

Pick small cucumbers for pickling about 5 days after the blossoms open.

**SING AND SHOUT AND DANCE ABOUT**
**THERE'S MAGIC IN THE BRUSSELS SPROUT**
**BOILED UP AND SERVED IN BUTTER**
**BAKED INTO A PIE**
**I LOVE TO EAT THE BRUSSELS SPROUT**
**TO BE WITHOUT WOULD MAKE ME CRY.**

–ROBERT CHAPLIN, CANADIAN ARTIST (B. 1968),
IN *BRUSSELS SPROUTS & UNICORNS*

The chill of a moderate frost or light snow improves the flavor of brussels sprouts, cabbage, carrots, kale, leeks, parsnips, and turnips.

Store apples separately from potatoes and other vegetables. The ethylene gas that apples release can shorten the storage life of other crops.

*Gardening is not intellectual; you must get out and do it.*

–Eudora Welty, American writer (1909–2001)

**PRESERVE YOUR MEMORIES,<br>KEEP THEM WELL,<br>WHAT YOU FORGET<br>YOU CAN NEVER RETELL.**

–LOUISA MAY ALCOTT,<br>AMERICAN WRITER (1832–88)

Illustrations by Kristin Kest for<br>*The Old Farmer's Almanac*



PRINTED IN MALAYSIA

ISBN: 978-1-961793-50-7